MW00973871

Self Explore
Self Restore

A Guided Self-Care Journal for Personal Growth and Reflection

By: G. Michelle White

Published by: Createspace

This journal is dedicated to survivors of unhealthy and abusive relationships. Thank you for your emotional dedication to finding healing. You all embody the true meaning of hope to me.

Your relationship with
yourself is precious and
valuable.

Intentions of this Journal:

My hope in creating this journal is to kindly and gently remind you that you have many tools within yourself to live a self-loving life. Taking care of you is essential and I hope that using this journal brings you a step closer to living a life that is pleasing to you.

In *Self Explore, Self Restore*, you will explore the many aspects of who you are, what you enjoy and how you would like to take care of yourself. You will also have the opportunity to restore and heal the parts of you that need extra care.

> *You are the expert of your experiences, your memories and your feelings about your relationships.*

With your internal strengths, you have the ability to restore and heal in your own way. This journal is here to help support your healing journey with you.

Though inspired by survivors of interpersonal trauma, **this journal is for any and all adults that would like to strengthen their self-care practice.**

Inspiration for this Journal:

This guided journal was inspired from my work in the field of interpersonal trauma, specifically working with survivors of domestic violence and child abuse.

In my roles as a licensed social worker, clinical therapist and professional trainer, I have encountered many stories of survivors feeling hurt, unappreciated and taken advantage of in unhealthy relationships. Personally, I am familiar with feeling less than my best self within former friendships and past intimate relationships.

> *Unhealthy and harmful relationships can have a significant impact on our emotional well-being and feelings about ourselves.*

These survivors have inspired me to create this journal to help:
- Reduce the shame and blame that folks can often feel when they are a part of *any* type of unhealthy relationship and;
- Increase feelings of worthiness and happiness through the exploration and restoration of self.

Practicing self-care is
essential to having a healthy
relationship with yourself.

What is Self-Care?

Self-care is *the intentional practice of identifying and caring for what you need, when you need it.*

Self-care can look different for everyone, but can typically include thinking of ways to fulfill your emotional, physical, social, spiritual and mental health needs.

Creating a self-care plan can be most beneficial when healing and recovering from unhealthy relationships. Thinking of ways to help you feel happy, satisfied, and relaxed ahead of time helps build our healthy coping skills and our ability to become resilient.

This journal is divided into four sections that explore how to:
- Recognize the love, care and appreciation of you
- Identify and utilize your inner strengths
- Engage in safe and healthy relationships with others
- Instill hope, positivity and gratitude into your self-care plan

This journal can become a part of your self-care plan, as well as a tool for healing.

7

Utilizing this Journal as a Healing Tool:

You are invited to use this journal at your own pace, on your own time. It is self-directed and centered on providing space for you to explore healing on your own terms.

There are a variety of ways you can utilize this journal as a tool for your healing journey:

- This journal can be used as a *self-assessment tool*, for you to see what areas of your healing you would like to spend more time on.

- This journal can be used as *a reference source* during and after you complete it to refer to when you need to care for yourself.

- This journal can also be used as *a space for self-care*, to increase your practice of mindfully pausing, allowing space to think and taking time for yourself.

Each prompt will invite you to think, write or draw a response. There are no wrong or right answers, just answers that are meaningful to you. Some prompts will ask you to list your answers and others will ask you to share your thoughts descriptively. You'll notice that some journal entries are shorter or longer than others.

There may be thoughts, feelings and memories that come up for you as you complete this journal. Take your time with each entry. Answer the questions and prompts that are suggested at your own discretion.

Some of the prompts may feel repetitive, while others may require more thought, time and patience. You can complete one entry at a time or choose to complete a few at once. Some entries may also include brief definitions and follow up questions to help add to your reflection process.

This journal was created with the intention that you can choose how you explore and restore yourself, in whatever way that feels right for you.

Special Considerations:

- Take your time with each journal entry

- If you find yourself stuck on a prompt or a question, give yourself permission to pause or come back to it.

- **If you are in an intimate relationship, friendship or family relationship that is unsafe, harmful or abusive, be mindful of your privacy and where you store this journal.**

- This journal is *not* intended to be a replacement or alternative to mental health care. Please connect with a licensed mental health professional if you are in need of more care and support for your healing.

Whether this is your first step towards practicing self-care or you are adding this journal to your self-care routine, I'm sending positive vibes and warm thoughts your way as you strengthen your ability to care for yourself.

With gratitude,

G. Michelle White

Table of Contents:

Getting Started ...

What motivated you to begin journaling?

_____

_____

_____

_____

_____

_____

_____

_____

_____

_____

_____

_____

_____

_____

_____

_____

What do you hope to take away from using your Self Explore, Self Restore journal?

_____

_____

_____

_____

_____

_____

_____

_____

_____

_____

_____

_____

_____

_____

_____

How will you know that you are getting closer to your goals?

_____

_____

_____

_____

_____

_____

_____

_____

_____

_____

_____

_____

_____

_____

_____

You are deserving of the love that you show to others.

Exploring the love, care and appreciation of you.

In this section, we will spend time honoring and reflecting on ways to appreciate the person that you are and your current self-care strategies.

Name 3 traits about yourself that you love:

1. _____

2. _____

3. _____

When you think about "loving yourself" what comes to your mind first?

_____

_____

_____

_____

_____

_____

_____

_____

What's your definition of "feeling proud"?

_____

_____

_____

_____

_____

_____

_____

Name 4 things that make you feel proud:

1. _____

2. _____

3. _____

4. _____

Devote a moment to appreciating a part of you that needs love, through words or drawing:

Write 4 things that give you joy:

1. _____

2. _____

3. _____

4. _____

List 3 songs that you love to move to:

1. _____

2. _____

3. _____

Think of 4 things that your inner child loves:

1. _____

2. _____

3. _____

4. _____

Do you have a
favorite memory,
game, experience
or activity from
childhood?

Describe the last time you celebrated yourself for doing something well:

_____

_____

_____

_____

_____

_____

_____

_____

_____

_____

_____

_____

_____

_____

_____

Create, draw or write your definition of
self-love ...

List 3 ways you would like to treat
yourself today:

1.

_____

_____

2.

_____

_____

3.

_____

_____

Write or draw one of your favorite traditions:

A tradition can be a ritual, gathering or activity that is special to you.

Choose 3 skills you are gifted with:

1.

_____

_____

2.

_____

_____

3.

_____

_____

Write a letter of love to yourself:
How do you show yourself love?

_____

_____

_____

_____

_____

_____

_____

_____

_____

_____

_____

_____

_____

_____

_____

_____

_____

_____

Recognize 3 parts of you that are unique from others:

1.

_____

2.

_____

3.

_____

What makes you different
from everyone else?

Write or draw your personal style:
Your personal style can include how you physically, socially or verbally express yourself

Recognize 3 parts of your culture that you are proud of:

1.

_____

_____

2.

_____

_____

3.

_____

_____

Describe what it looks like when you feel confident. What do you notice about you?

_____
_____
_____
_____
_____
_____
_____
_____
_____
_____
_____
_____
_____
_____
_____
_____

Describe, write or draw what gives you comfort.

What helps you feel relaxed and stress-free?

Recognize 5 ways you take care of your body every day:

1. _____
   _____

2. _____
   _____

3. _____
   _____

4. _____
   _____

5. _____
   _____

Write a letter to your younger self:

What would your younger self need to hear from you now?

_____

_____

_____

_____

_____

_____

_____

_____

_____

_____

_____

_____

_____

_____

_____

_____

Think of 4 of your favorite ways to spend a day off:

1. _____
   _____
   _____

2. _____
   _____
   _____

3. _____
   _____
   _____

4. _____
   _____
   _____

Describe a time when you felt adventurous, through drawing or writing:

When was the last time you had a remarkable or exciting experience? How did you feel?

Reflect on 4 ways you care for yourself in a working role:

(As a student, as a parent, as a working person ...)

1. _____
   _____
   _____

2. _____
   _____
   _____

3. _____
   _____
   _____

4. _____
   _____
   _____

Describe how you like to celebrate your culture, through writing or drawing:

How do you enjoy
expressing your
culture?

Reflect on how you connect with your intimate needs:

Your intimate needs include your sensual interests and sexual desires.

_____

_____

_____

_____

_____

_____

_____

_____

_____

_____

_____

_____

_____

_____

_____

_____

_____

Think of 3 ways you show love to your body:

1.

_____

_____

2.

_____

_____

3.

_____

_____

Describe what spirituality and faith means to you.

_____

_____

_____

_____

_____

_____

_____

_____

_____

_____

_____

_____

_____

_____

_____

_____

*How do you define being
spiritual or faithful?*

You are capable and able of taking care of you.

Exploring how to identify and utilize your inner strengths.

In this section, we will take a look at the skills, strengths and abilities you have to practice your self-care strategies when you need them.

Reflect on 4 practices that help you feel calm:

1. _____
   _____
   _____

2. _____
   _____
   _____

3. _____
   _____
   _____

4. _____
   _____
   _____

Think of 3 smells that help you feel peaceful:

1.

_____

2.

_____

3.

_____

Lavender and lemon are scents associated with feeling relaxed.

What's your definition of "feeling strong"?

_____
_____
_____
_____
_____
_____
_____
_____

List 3 things that help you feel strong:

1. _____

2. _____

3. _____

Think of 4 ways you practice self-reflection:

How do you like to take time to pause and think about your behaviors, beliefs and experiences?

1. _____
   _____
   _____

2. _____
   _____
   _____

3. _____
   _____
   _____

4. _____
   _____
   _____

Describe 3 ways you can hold yourself accountable:

1. _____
   _____
   _____

2. _____
   _____
   _____

3. _____
   _____
   _____

Being accountable can mean being willing to accept responsibility

Reflect on the last time
you were flexible:
When was the last time you were able to positively adapt to something new or different?

_____

_____

_____

_____

_____

_____

_____

_____

_____

_____

_____

_____

_____

Name 3 of your core values:

1. _____
_____
_____

2. _____
_____
_____

3. _____
_____
_____

Your core values are
personal principles that
shape your beliefs.

Describe how you like to start your day,
through writing or drawing:

Practicing a morning routine can
help us feel more organized.

Recognize 3 ways you know that you are growing:

1. _____
_____
_____

2. _____
_____
_____

3. _____
_____
_____

What does it look
like when you're
making changes?

Think of 4 ways you can take care of yourself that are cost-free:

1. _____
   _____
   _____

2. _____
   _____
   _____

3. _____
   _____
   _____

4. _____
   _____
   _____

Describe a time when you bounced back from a tough situation:

_____

_____

_____

_____

_____

_____

_____

_____

_____

_____

_____

_____

Resiliency:
The ability to recover from or adjust
easily to misfortune or change

Write or draw how you take care of
your 5 senses.

Recognize 3 things that help you feel balanced:

1. _____
   _____
   _____

2. _____
   _____
   _____

3. _____
   _____
   _____

What helps you feel centered or focused?

Describe what it looks like when you are
patient with yourself,
through writing or drawing:

Name 3 things that help you feel brave:

1. _____
_____
_____

2. _____
_____
_____

3. _____
_____
_____

What helps you
feel courageous?

List 3 habits that you currently practice that you consider healthy:

1. _____
   _____
   _____
   _____

2. _____
   _____
   _____
   _____

3. _____
   _____
   _____
   _____

Think of 4 ways you would like to take a break:

1. _____
   _____
   _____

2. _____
   _____
   _____

3. _____
   _____
   _____

4. _____
   _____
   _____

List 3 ways you would like to reward yourself after accomplishing a goal:

1. _____
_____
_____
_____

2. _____
_____
_____
_____

3. _____
_____
_____
_____

Describe that last time you emotionally protected yourself, through writing or drawing:

Protecting your emotions can include standing up for yourself or removing yourself from an emotionally unsafe environment

Think of 3 things that instantly cheer you up:

1. _____
   _____
   _____

2. _____
   _____
   _____

3. _____
   _____
   _____

What helps you
feel better
quickly?

Write or draw how you prepare to relax or sleep:

Describe 3 practices that help you feel organized:

1. _____
   _____
   _____
   _____

2. _____
   _____
   _____
   _____

3. _____
   _____
   _____
   _____

Our relationships with others can reflect our relationship with ourselves.

Exploring how to engage in safe, healthy and satisfying relationships.

In this section, we will reflect on what your needs are in your relationships and how to identify your support system.

Reflect on 3 boundaries that you maintain in your relationships with others:

1. _____
   _____
   _____

2. _____
   _____
   _____

3. _____
   _____
   _____

Boundary: setting a limit or
expectation to keep yourself safe

Name 3 people whom you trust:

1. _____

2. _____

3. _____

What's trustworthy about the people you have chosen?

_____
_____
_____
_____
_____
_____
_____
_____
_____
_____

Name 3 people whom regularly show you compassion:

1.

_____

2.

_____

3.

_____

Compassion: sympathetic
consciousness of others' distress,
with a desire to alleviate it

Name 4 traits you appreciate in a caring friend:

1. _____

2. _____

3. _____

4. _____

Who comes to mind when you think of a caring friend? How come?

_____

_____

_____

_____

_____

_____

Think of 3 ways you prefer to be appreciated by others:

1. _____
   _____
   _____
   _____

2. _____
   _____
   _____
   _____

3. _____
   _____
   _____
   _____

Reflect on the signs you are in a safe relationship or friendship:

Safety in a relationship can include thinking about your physical, mental and emotional safety.

_____

_____

_____

_____

_____

_____

_____

_____

_____

_____

_____

_____

_____

_____

_____

_____

Think of 4 ways you know you are
receiving positive support from someone:

1.

_____
_____
_____

2. _____
_____
_____

3. _____
_____
_____

4. _____
_____
_____

By writing or drawing, describe what it looks like when you need the support of a loved one:

Name 3 people you talk to when you
have good news:

1. _____

2. _____

3. _____

What do you like about telling these
folks about your good news?

_____
_____
_____
_____
_____
_____
_____
_____
_____

Name 4 ways you show your loyalty:

1. _____
   _____
   _____

2. _____
   _____
   _____

3. _____
   _____
   _____

4. _____
   _____
   _____

Describe what you need to feel emotionally safe with others:

_____

_____

_____

_____

_____

_____

_____

_____

_____

_____

_____

_____

_____

_____

_____

Name 3 people you enjoy receiving advice or guidance from:

1. _____

2. _____

3. _____

What boundaries do you have around receiving advice from others?

_____

_____

_____

_____

_____

_____

_____

_____

Write or draw about a time you were able to clearly communicate what you needed:

How did you know you were communicating clearly?

Describe what it means for you to trust someone:

_____

_____

_____

_____

_____

_____

_____

_____

_____

_____

_____

_____

_____

_____

_____

_____

_____

What does trust mean to you?

List 3 things you need in a healthy intimate relationship:

1. _____
_____
_____
_____

2. _____
_____
_____
_____

3. _____
_____
_____
_____

Describe the last time you told someone "no":

When was the last time you maintained your boundaries?

_____

_____

_____

_____

_____

_____

_____

_____

_____

_____

_____

_____

_____

_____

_____

Name 3 things you love about your
closest loved one:

1. _____
   _____
   _____
   _____

2. _____
   _____
   _____
   _____

3. _____
   _____
   _____
   _____

Describe how you receive energy from others. Are you an introvert, an extrovert, or an ambivert?

_____

_____

_____

_____

_____

_____

_____

_____

_____

_____

_____

_____

Do you recharge by spending time alone, being with others or both?

Name 4 people in your life whom share
your similar core values:

1.

_____

2.

_____

3.

_____

4.

_____

*With hope, we can envision
a bright future for ourselves.*

*Exploring how to instill hope, gratitude
and positivity into your self-care plan.*

*In this section, we will take a step forward
into how to care for your future self, using
an encouraging and optimistic lens.*

Think of 3 things you can do this week
to make your future-self happy:

1. _____
   _____
   _____
   _____

2. _____
   _____
   _____
   _____

3. _____
   _____
   _____
   _____

What does your future-self need
later today? Tomorrow?

Create an affirmation that is meaningful
to you.

Name 3 goals you would like to
accomplish:

1. _____
   _____
   _____
   _____

2. _____
   _____
   _____
   _____

3. _____
   _____
   _____
   _____

Write or draw how you would like to be remembered:

What impression would you like to make on others?

_____

_____

_____

_____

_____

_____

_____

_____

_____

_____

_____

_____

_____

Reflect on 3 parts of your day that you
feel grateful for:

1. _____
_____
_____
_____

2. _____
_____
_____
_____

3. _____
_____
_____
_____

*Gratitude: Feeling
thankful or appreciative*

Describe what it means for you to be hopeful:
What does hope mean to you?

_____

_____

_____

_____

_____

_____

_____

_____

_____

_____

_____

_____

_____

_____

_____

Think of 4 things you are hopeful for:

1. _____
   _____
   _____

2. _____
   _____
   _____

3. _____
   _____
   _____

4. _____
   _____
   _____

Describe the last time you felt motivated:

_____

_____

_____

_____

_____

_____

_____

_____

_____

_____

_____

_____

_____

Name 5 ways you would like to be encouraged:

1. _____

   _____

2. _____

   _____

3. _____

   _____

4. _____

   _____

5. _____

   _____

Reflect on 3 things that inspire you.

1. _____
   _____
   _____
   _____

2. _____
   _____
   _____
   _____

3. _____
   _____
   _____
   _____

Describe a childhood dream that is still meaningful to you today:

_____
_____
_____
_____
_____
_____
_____
_____
_____
_____
_____
_____
_____
_____
_____
_____

Think of 4 things that help you feel motivated:

1. _____
_____
_____

2. _____
_____
_____

3. _____
_____
_____

4. _____
_____
_____

Reflect on 3 ways you can refocus:

1. _____
_____
_____
_____

2. _____
_____
_____
_____

3. _____
_____
_____
_____

Envision the happiest and healthiest version of yourself:

What does it mean for you to be healthy? What does "being happy and healthy" look like for you?

Completing this Journal ...

If you have completed the prompts in this journal, how would you like to celebrate?

_____

_____

_____

_____

_____

_____

_____

_____

_____

_____

_____

What was it like for you to reflect on the prompts provided in this journal? What came up for you?

_____

_____

_____

_____

_____

_____

_____

_____

_____

_____

_____

_____

_____

Is there anything you would like to change about this experience? If so, what would you like to change?

_____
_____
_____
_____
_____
_____
_____
_____
_____
_____
_____
_____

What's the next step for your self-care journey? What would you like to do to continue taking care of yourself?

_____

_____

_____

_____

_____

_____

_____

_____

_____

_____

_____

_____

Write what you may need to continue
your self-care journey here:

_____

_____

_____

_____

_____

_____

_____

_____

_____

_____

_____

_____

_____

About the Author:

G. Michelle White is a licensed social worker and professional trainer. She has worked in the domestic violence and child abuse fields as a clinical therapist to help adults, children and families heal from the trauma of their interpersonal relationships. She has developed and facilitated community and statewide trainings on domestic violence through managing the first Child & Youth Project with the Georgia Coalition Against Domestic Violence.

While her first name is Gennifer, in her everyday life she goes by her middle name Michelle. Michelle enjoys listening to podcasts, spending time with her loved ones and finding new ways to take care of herself while residing in Atlanta, Georgia. Follow Michelle on social media platforms at @thegmichelle and visit her website at www.gmichelle.com.

Made in the USA
Columbia, SC
29 July 2024

39043958R00059